Music Genres

Classical Music

by Meg Thacher

FOCUS READERS

BEACON

www.focusreaders.com

Focus Readers is distributed by North Star Editions:
sales@northstareditions.com | 888-417-0195

Produced for Focus Readers by Red Line Editorial.

Photographs ©: Vit Simanek/CTK/AP Images, cover, 1; David A. Beloff/Getty Images Entertainment/Getty Images, 4; Paras Griffin/Getty Images Entertainment/Getty Images, 7; Mark Sagliocco/Getty Images Entertainment/Getty Images, 8; Shutterstock Images, 11, 13, 14, 17, 22, 27, 29; Brownie Harris/Corbis Historical/Getty Images, 19; Bilal Hussein/AP Images, 20–21; Stephen J. Cohen/Getty Images Entertainment/Getty Images, 25

Library of Congress Cataloging-in-Publication Data
Names: Thacher, Meg, author.
Title: Classical music / Meg Thacher.
Description: Mendota Heights, MN: Focus Readers, 2025. | Series: Music genres | Includes index. | Audience: Grades 2-3
Identifiers: LCCN 2023051863 (print) | LCCN 2023051864 (ebook) | ISBN 9798889981985 (hardcover) | ISBN 9798889982548 (paperback) | ISBN 9798889983620 (pdf) | ISBN 9798889983101 (ebook)
Subjects: LCSH: Music--History and criticism--Juvenile literature.
Classification: LCC ML3928 .T43 2025 (print) | LCC ML3928 (ebook) | DDC 780.9--dc23/eng/20231103
LC record available at https://lccn.loc.gov/2023051863
LC ebook record available at https://lccn.loc.gov/2023051864

Printed in the United States of America
Mankato, MN
082024

About the Author

Meg Thacher writes nonfiction articles and books, mostly about science. She has played piano and a bit of guitar, clarinet, and harp, but she likes singing best. She has sung in professional and amateur choirs for 50 years. She enjoyed listening to a lot of classical music while writing this book.

Table of Contents

Chapter 1

A Musical Bumblebee

Eighty musicians sit on a stage. They are in a huge concert hall. The **conductor** steps onto a platform. The audience is silent. The conductor raises her arms.

One job of the conductor is to show musicians how loud or soft to play.

The music starts with a crash of **percussion**. First, the violins play a **melody**. The notes swoop up and down. Next, the conductor points to the flutes. It is their turn to play the melody. The violins buzz. The music sounds like a bumblebee.

Did You Know?

Bands and orchestras are both groups of musicians. Orchestras include string instruments. Bands focus on wind instruments instead.

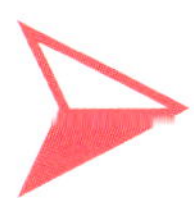

A violin is played by moving a bow across the instrument's strings.

The conductor bounces and sways. She waves her hands with a steady **rhythm**. The orchestra follows her beat. The music ends. The crowd claps and cheers.

Chapter 2

What Is Classical Music?

The term *classical music* describes music based on traditions from **Western** art. Classical music is known for being complex. It is usually performed by groups. But solo musicians can play it, too.

Classical music is often performed in concert halls.

Some classical performers sing. Others play **acoustic** instruments. These instruments are grouped into different families. Percussion instruments make sounds when they are hit. Drums and cymbals are two examples.

Another family of instruments uses strings to make sounds. Musicians can strum or pluck the strings. Or they can move bows across them. Violins and guitars are stringed instruments.

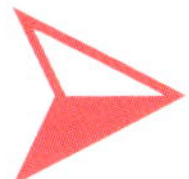

Timpani are large drums played with mallets.

Wind instruments are another family. They make sounds when players blow into them. This family is split into two sections. One is woodwinds. It includes clarinets and flutes. The other is brass. It includes trumpets and tubas.

Works of classical music can be long. Many works are made up of several sections. These parts are called movements. Symphonies often last for more than an hour. They usually have four movements. Each movement has different sounds and melodies.

Flutes are made of metal. But they are in the woodwind family. Early flutes were made of wood.

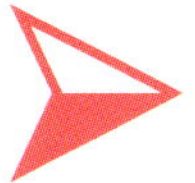

Sheet music is a common form of musical notation.

Classical music is usually written down. It uses a system called musical notation. Notation shows musicians what notes to play. It also shows how the music should feel. For example, it tells how fast or loud notes should be.

Chapter 3

Classical Music History

Classical music started in the Middle Ages. This period lasted from the 400s to the 1400s CE. During that time, European monks started writing their music down. The songs had simple melodies.

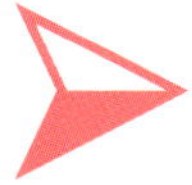

Some monks wrote music for pipe organs.

Most songs had just one or two voice parts.

The Renaissance Period came next. It took place from 1400 to 1600. In this period, several voices and instruments played together. They created a blended sound.

The Baroque Period lasted from 1600 to 1750. Baroque music was often showy. Johann Sebastian Bach wrote music during this time.

The Classical Period followed. It went from 1750 to 1830. Its music

Many people believe Johann Sebastian Bach was one of the greatest composers of all time.

tended to feature one main melody. It also followed strict forms. For example, sonatas often had three parts. Wolfgang Amadeus Mozart wrote many famous sonatas. He also wrote **operas** and other forms.

The Romantic Period lasted from 1830 to 1900. Romantic music tended to be dramatic. It showed lots of emotion. **Composers** often wrote about feelings and nature. Ludwig van Beethoven was one example. His Ninth Symphony ends with sounds that show joy.

Many cultures have their own classical music. For example, Chinese opera is hundreds of years old.

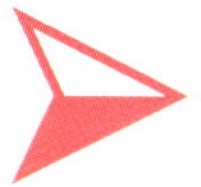

Philip Glass became a famous composer in the late 1900s. He wrote music with lots of repetition.

In the 1900s, composers threw out all the rules. Some went back to older styles. But many used new and unusual harmonies and rhythms. People also borrowed ideas from other music styles.

ARTIST SPOTLIGHT

Yo-Yo Ma

Yo-Yo Ma is one of the world's most famous classical musicians. He plays cello. He started when he was only four years old. As an adult, Ma has won many awards. He often plays with famous orchestras. But he enjoys many kinds of music. For example, he plays with jazz and folk musicians. He uses music to bring people together.

In 1998, Ma formed a group called Silkroad. This group plays classical music from many cultures. It helps **preserve** traditional music styles.

Yo-Yo Ma has recorded more than 90 albums.

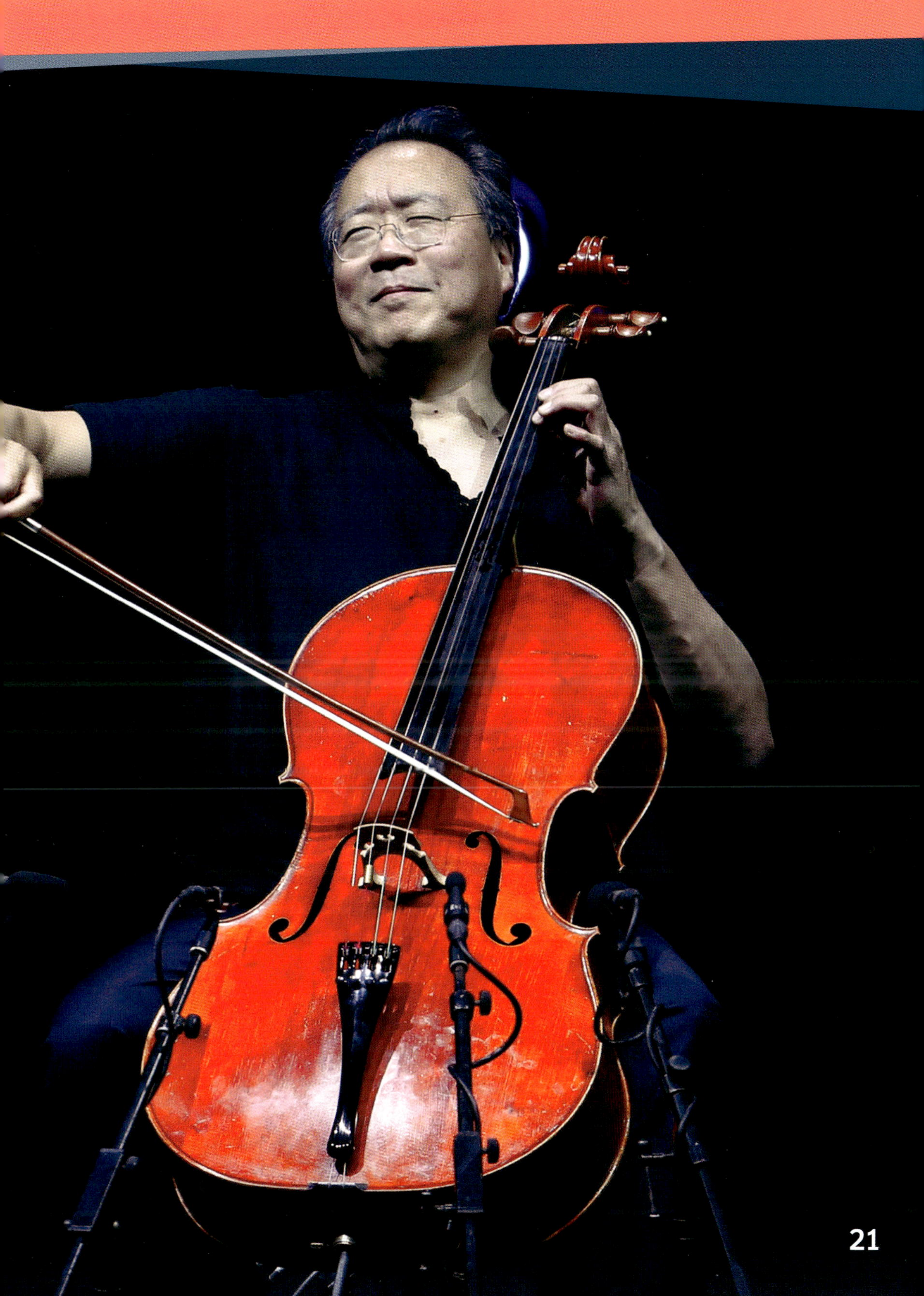

Chapter 4

Classical Music Today

Today's classical music is a mix of old and new. Many older pieces are still being played today. And some composers still copy old forms or sounds. But modern composers continue to try new things.

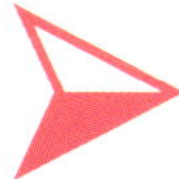

Orchestras often have several people playing each instrument.

Some composers use electric instruments. Others blend in other musical styles. For instance, some performers mix classical music and pop. A group called Black Violin blends classical music and hip-hop.

Classical concerts are often formal. Musicians wear fancy clothes. Audiences sit quietly. They do not dance or sing along. But many musicians are trying to change that. They want everyone to enjoy classical concerts. So, they

The musicians in Black Violin have been playing together since 2004.

make some concerts more casual. Orchestras often hold concerts for families with children. They may play outdoors at parks. Or they may have programs for schools.

Long ago, most performers were European men. But today, classical musicians come from a wide variety of backgrounds. Many people take lessons. They learn to play and write music.

Classical music can be found many places. It is taught in schools.

In 2006, a composer wrote a piece for cell phones. Audience members played their ringtones during the concert.

Hundreds of people gather for a classical music performance in a park.

It plays on the radio. Streaming services have classical playlists. Many movies use classical music, too. It helps create emotions. In all these ways, classical music remains important.

FOCUS ON

Classical Music

Write your answers on a separate piece of paper.

1. Write a paragraph explaining the main ideas of Chapter 2.
2. Which period of classical music do you find most interesting? Why?
3. How many movements does a symphony usually have?
   - A. two
   - B. four
   - C. nine
4. Which of these periods happened first?
   - A. Romantic Period
   - B. Baroque Period
   - C. Renaissance Period

5. What does **solo** mean in this book?

It is usually performed by groups. But ***solo*** *musicians can play it, too.*

A. playing in a large group
B. performing alone
C. too old to play

6. What does **formal** mean in this book?

Classical concerts are often ***formal****. Musicians wear fancy clothes. Audiences sit quietly.*

A. having a style that follows the rules
B. having a style that ignores the rules
C. having a style that changes often

Answer key on page 32.

Glossary

acoustic
Not electric.

composers
People who write music.

conductor
The leader of an orchestra.

melody
The tune of a piece of music.

operas
Plays where actors sing instead of speaking.

percussion
Instruments played by being hit or shaken, such as drums or bells.

preserve
To make sure something keeps happening, or to make sure something does not go away.

rhythm
A regular beat.

Western
Related to countries in Western Europe and North America.

To Learn More

BOOKS

Auld, Mary. *How to Build an Orchestra.* Northampton, MA: Crocodile Books, 2020.

Gieseke, Tyler. *Orchestra.* Minneapolis: Abdo Publishing, 2023.

Worthey, Diane. *In One Ear and Out the Other: Antonia Brico and Her Amazingly Musical Life.* Oklahoma City: Penny Candy Books, 2020.

NOTE TO EDUCATORS

Visit **www.focusreaders.com** to find lesson plans, activities, links, and other resources related to this title.

Index

Answer Key: 1. Answers will vary; **2.** Answers will vary; **3.** B; **4.** C; **5.** B; **6.** A